A SMART START READER

OWLS

Photo credits:

ISBN: 0-439-23780-7

OWLS

by
Nancy Ellwood

Scholastic Inc.
New York • Toronto • London • Auckland • Sydney
Mexico City • New Delhi • Hong Kong

What Are Owls?

Owls are birds that live on every continent in the world except Antarctica. They live in many different **habitats:** deserts, prairies, forests, and even the Arctic **tundra**. No matter where owls live, they are known for two things: their large, round eyes, and the "hoot, hoot, hoot!" sounds that they make at night.

Many Different Owls

▲ Great horned owl

◄ Elf owl

Eagle ▲ owl

Spectacled owl ▶

There are more than 162 **species,** or types, of owls. The largest type is the eagle owl, which grows to a little over two feet. The smallest is the elf owl, which grows no larger than five or six inches. Besides size, owls also vary in their coloring and in shape of face or head feathers.

▶ Saw-whet owl

Barn ▶ owl

Malay or buffy fish owl ▶

Useful Colors

Many owls have brown or gray feathers that help them blend in with their surroundings. The snowy owl, which lives in the Arctic, has white feathers that blend in with the snow. Coloring that helps an animal hide is called **camouflage.**

Owl Homes

Owls rarely build nests. Usually, they move into nests left by other animals or birds. Most owls live in hollow trees. Barn owls live in barns and empty buildings. Screech owls and saw-whet owls live in giant desert cactuses. Burrowing owls, like the one below, live under the ground, in tunnels and holes dug by other animals. Sometimes, they dig new burrows with their sharp **talons** and long, powerful legs.

Big Eyes

The owl's large, round eyes are special. Unlike other birds' eyes, an owl's eyes are on the front of its face, not the sides of its head. This gives the owl very good eyesight. However, an owl can't move its eyes in its eye sockets the way people can. In order to see what is going on around it, an owl can turn its head all the way to the back, and then some, like the owl at right.

Night Owls

Owl eyes are specially **adapted** for seeing at night. This is very important, because owls are **nocturnal** animals. They spend much of the day sleeping and much of the night hunting. They can't see colors, but they can see very well in the dark. Their eyes are sensitive to light—even dim light from the moon and stars. In fact, owls can see better in the dark than they can in daylight.

Silent Fliers

Owls are **raptors,** or birds of **prey.** This means that they hunt for food. Their good eyesight and hearing make them very good hunters. The snowy owl can hear a mouse burrowing under snow and earth! Owls also have very soft, fluffy feathers that absorb sound. This allows them to swoop down and grab prey without making any noise.

Hunting Tools

Silent wings are not the owl's only hunting tool. This bird is also equipped with mighty talons and a sharp beak. The owl uses its talons to catch prey and its beak to carry the prey back to the nest. There, the owl usually eats the prey in one big gulp! If the prey is too large, however, the owl will use its talons and scissorlike beak to tear its meal into pieces.

Dinner Time!

Owls are most likely to eat mice, rats, frogs, insects, snakes, and small birds. Some owls catch and eat fish. The main prey in an owl's diet usually depends on the size of the owl and where it lives.

The owl below has caught a small fish. The owl in the center is eating a garter snake, and the owl at far right is about to eat a woodpecker.

This screech owl mother is keeping her eggs warm.

Owl Families

Some owls, such as the screech owl, stay with one mate for years. Other types of owl have different mates. At least once a year—usually in late winter or early spring—the female lays up to 10 eggs in the nest. She will sit on the eggs for about three to five weeks. This **incubates** them, or keeps them warm, until they hatch.

This baby screech owl is only one day old.

Baby Owls

When the eggs hatch, out come blind, fuzzy, baby owls, called **owlets.** After the owlets are born, the mother owl brings food to them. Sometimes, she will bring small insects for the owlets to eat whole. Other times, she brings larger prey that she tears into small bits to feed to her babies.

These little barn owlets are only a few days old.

Moving Out

Owlets learn to fly when they are about two months old. Soon after their first flight, they move out. The owlets are then old enough to find their own nests and hunt by themselves. After a few months to a year, an owl may find a mate and start its own family.

Learning About Owls

An owl can't digest everything that it eats. Its body can't break down fur, bones, and teeth, for instance. So the owl coughs those things up in a lump called a **pellet.** We have learned a great deal about owls by studying their pellets.

Owls & Us

Owls have few **predators** in the wild. The biggest threat they face comes from people, whose activities may disturb the trees, cactuses, or burrows where owls live. But people often work to help save owls, too—by building them homes, for example, or caring for hurt owls until they can care for themselves.

Glossary

Adapt (uh-DAPT): Change to fit one's surroundings

Camouflage (KAM-uh-flahj): Markings on an animal's feathers, skin, or fur that help it blend in with its surroundings.

Habitat (HAB-uh-tat): The surroundings in which an animal lives.

Incubate (ING-kyoo-bate): To keep warm.

Nocturnal (nahk-TURN-ul): Active at night.

Owlet (OW-let): A baby owl.

Predator (PRED-uh-tur): An animal that kills other animals for food.

Pellet (PELL-ut): A lump of material that an owl coughs up, containing fur, bones, teeth, and other things that its body can't digest.

Prey (PRAY): Animals that are hunted

Raptor (RAP-tur): A bird that hunts other animals.

Species (SPEE-sheez): A type of animal or plant.

Talons (TAHL-unz): The strong claws of an owl or other bird of prey.

Tundra (TUN-druh): A cold, treeless area with muddy or frozen ground.